Gravity

GRAVITY

Simple Experiments for Young Scientists

Larry White

illustrated by Laurie Hamilton

The Millbrook Press
Brookfield, Connecticut

I have written over 20 books and
never dedicated one to my wife, Doris.
As my wife of 30+ years she has
controlled gravity . . . keeping me
"down to Earth"!

This book is for you, Doris.

Published by The Millbrook Press
2 Old New Milford Road, Brookfield, Connecticut 06804

Copyright © 1995 by Larry White
Printed in the United States of America
1   3   5   4   2

Library of Congress Cataloging-in-Publication Data
White, Laurence B.
Gravity : simple experiments for young scientists / by Larry White.
p.   cm.
Includes bibliographical references and index.
ISBN 1-56294-470-3
1. Gravitation—Juvenile literature.   2. Gravity—Measurement—
Experiments—Juvenile literature.   [1. Gravity—Experiments.
2. Experiments.]   I. Title.   II. Series.
QC178.W458   1995   531′.14′078—dc20   94-9838   CIP   AC

Here's a challenge: Throw a ball in the air. Throw the ball so it travels in a straight line for about 10 feet (30 meters) and comes to a complete stop. Then it should change direction and travel in a straight line back to your hand! Can you do it?

What if you throw the ball in a straight line to a friend standing 10 feet away? Couldn't your friend stop the ball by catching it and throw it back? Wouldn't the ball then travel in a straight line back to your hand?

The answer is no. And the reason is **gravity**. Gravity is a **force** that pulls things downward. A force is a push or pull on an object. Because of gravity you cannot throw the ball in a straight line to your friend. You have to throw the ball slightly upward, because gravity will pull the ball downward as it travels to your friend. And your friend has to throw the ball slightly upward back to you for the same reason. So, as long as there is gravity, there is no way you can throw a ball in a straight line — or is there?

Yes there is! And, to solve the challenge of throwing the ball in a straight line, having it stop, and return to your hand, all you have to do is use gravity. You can throw a ball in a straight line if you throw it directly *up*. Think about what happens when you do this. As the ball travels upward, gravity pulls on it, drawing it downward. After the ball travels a short distance, gravity wins. The ball stops, reverses direction, and falls in a straight line back to your hand.

An Attractive Force

Gravity is, as we have said, a force. Other forces are electricity and magnetism. Magnetism is a force you may have experience with. It is the force most like gravity. Magnets attract certain kinds of metal and other magnets. Like magnetism, gravity has been called an attractive force. Earth's gravity attracts everything to the ground. If it didn't, everything on Earth would go flying into space.

Gravity Is Everywhere

No matter where you travel on Earth, you will find gravity. If you pick up a big rock or the tiniest grain of sand, and drop it, gravity will pull it back down to the ground. And, of course, no matter where you are, gravity holds you down on Earth too.

Gravity holds buildings, plants, animals, water, automobiles, and everything else down. If you want to understand how gravity works, you have to learn what the word *down* means!

Down With Giants

Needed:

a piece of paper

a pencil

1. Draw a big circle on the piece of paper. Pretend this is our planet Earth and you are looking at it from space. Pretend there are giant people living on Earth. Draw a giant, like the one in Figure 1 (page 8), on top of Earth. (This would be the North Pole.) Be sure you draw the giant so the feet are *down*, touching the ground, the way people stand.

2. Now draw another giant beside this one. Point the feet down too. Continue drawing giants until you have drawn them all around the world. Now look at a giant on one side of the drawing and look at a giant directly opposite on the other side. Imagine that you can move them together and they meet in the middle of Earth. Their feet would be touching! (See Figure 2, page 8.)

Figure 1

Figure 2

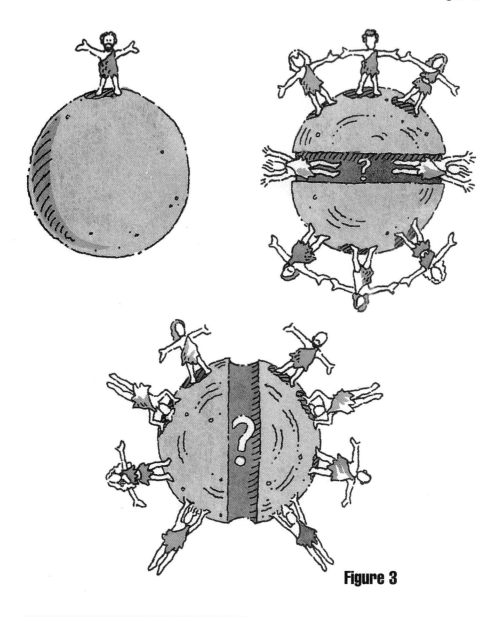

Figure 3

No matter where you go, a person on the other side of the world will be opposite you in this way. Can you and your opposite ever both be facing down in the same way, so that if you meet in the middle of Earth one's feet would touch the other's head? (See Figure 3.) The English scientist Sir Isaac Newton considered those questions. And some say he learned the answers to them from an apple tree.

What Did Sir Isaac Newton Learn From an Apple Tree?

Sir Isaac Newton was born on Christmas 1642 and died in 1727, when he was nearly 85 years old. During his lifetime he made many discoveries that help us understand how our world works. Sir Isaac Newton is also often the first scientist children learn about because of the "apple tree story."

One day Sir Isaac was sitting by an apple tree, and he saw an apple fall. Some say that the apple fell on his head! But that is probably made up just to make the story more fun. The important part is that watching the apple fall got Sir Isaac thinking about gravity and, most important, about the word *down*.

He probably imagined our world much the way you drew it, except with apple trees instead of giants. In his mind, no matter where a tree was on Earth its apples always fell to the

Figure 3

ground. But, if an apple from a tree at the North Pole fell down, would an apple from a tree at the South Pole fall up? (Look at your drawing again and think about that!) And how about apples from trees growing at the equator—would they fall sideways?

If all the apples on Earth fall down, Sir Isaac reasoned, then "down" must be toward the center of Earth. Indeed it is!

A Hole Through Earth

Imagine if a hole were drilled from the North Pole all the way through the world to the South Pole and you jumped in the hole. What would happen? You would drop all the way through the hole, then turn around and drop through in the other direction, then turn around again and fall back the other way, over and over until gravity finally made you stop. Where would you finally stop? You would stop at "down," the exact center of Earth!

Everything Has Its Own Gravity

After explaining what the word *down* means, Sir Isaac Newton thought about the fact that gravity is everywhere on Earth. He believed that every object has its own gravity too.

Then he described how he thought all the planets, moons, and stars attract each other, with their gravities. He called this the **universal law of gravity**.

Why Does the Moon Go Around the Earth?

Without gravity, the moon would fly into space. Earth's gravity draws the moon toward Earth's center, and the moon's gravity draws Earth toward the moon's center. Because of these forces, the moon cannot fly into space.

At the same time, the moon is moving. It moves in a straight line in space. But if the moon moves in a straight line, how can it circle Earth? While the moon is moving, Earth's gravity pulls at the moon. This pull makes the moon circle, or orbit, Earth and prevents the two from crashing together. You can see how this happens with a simple experiment.

Make the Moon Fly Away

Needed:

paper towel

piece of string 5 feet (1.5 meters) long

tape

1. Crumple up the paper towel to make a soft ball. Wrap tape around the crumpled towel so that it keeps its round shape. Tape one end of the string to the ball. Hold the opposite end of the string and spin the ball around your body. (See Figure 4.)

Figure 4

2. Pretend that the ball is the moon, your body is Earth, and the string is gravity. As long as you hold the string, the ball is forced to go around you. As long as gravity exists, the moon is forced to go around Earth.

3. Now let go of the string. The ball immediately stops going around and flies away from you. If gravity suddenly "turned off," the moon would do exactly the same thing as the paper ball.

At the center of our solar system is the sun. All of the planets spin around the sun. The sun's gravity attracts the planets, and each planet's gravity attracts the sun in exactly the same way. So the planets will circle the sun forever, and never be able to break away. Throughout space, other planets circle other stars and some stars even circle other stars—all because of the universal law of gravity, which states that every body possesses gravity.

The Moon Has Gravity

Now you know if you go to the moon you won't fly off. Your feet will stay down. But in this case "down" means toward the center of the moon, because the moon has its own gravity. Is the pull of gravity on the moon the same as on Earth? To find out, we can measure the pull of gravity on Earth and compare it to the pull of gravity on the moon.

How can we measure the pull of gravity on Earth?

Weighing In on Earth and the Moon

Needed:

a bathroom scale

a pencil

a piece of paper

1. When you step on the scale, gravity pulls you downward against the scale. You can read this pull as pounds. How many pounds do you weigh? Look at the scale and write down your weight.

2. Now consider your weight in relation to the moon. The moon is only one fourth as large as Earth. The **mass**, or amount of matter of any object, determines its gravity. Since the moon has less mass than Earth, it does not have as much gravity. If you took your bathroom scale to the moon, you would be surprised to find that you weigh only between one fourth and one sixth of what you weigh on Earth. (Gravity varies somewhat from place to place on the moon. Scientists are not sure why.) If you took your scale to Jupiter, the largest planet, you would weigh two and a half times more than you do on Earth. Why? The answer is simple: The larger an object is, the more gravity it has.

The sun is a star a million times larger than Earth. What do you suppose you would weigh if you could go there? A little arithmetic can tell you your approximate weight on any object in space.

Want to Be a Space Traveler? Watch Your Weight!

Needed:

paper

pencil

a pocket calculator (optional)

1. Pretend you are going to visit the sun, the moon, and each planet in our solar system. You want to know ahead of time how much you will weigh on each.

2. Use the following formulas and divide if the place you want to visit is smaller than Earth, or multiply if it is larger.

This will give you your approximate weight on the place you wish to travel to.

Astronaut's Weight-Planning Table

Earth weight divided by 7.5 = weight on Pluto
Earth weight divided by 2.9 = weight on Mercury
Earth weight divided by 2.63 = weight on Mars
Earth weight divided by 1.15 = weight on Venus
Earth weight multiplied by 1.06 = weight on Uranus
Earth weight multiplied by 1.13 = weight on Saturn
Earth weight multiplied by 1.4 = weight on Neptune
Earth weight multiplied by 2.63 = weight on Jupiter
Earth weight multiplied by 279 = weight on the sun

What Is "Weightlessness"?

Perhaps you are saying, "I thought people in space were weightless." You have seen pictures of astronauts floating around in the spaceship cabin. But gravity is pulling on these astronauts, just as it pulls on you. Why then do they appear to be weightless?

Here's one way to understand weightlessness: Suppose you took your bathroom scale on an elevator and the elevator went to the top floor and stopped. If you stood on your scale, you would read your correct weight on the dial. But now imagine the elevator started to fall downward at extraordinary speed—faster than an actual elevator could fall—with you in it. While you were falling, the scale would read zero, and if you lifted your legs you would appear to float in the air. All that is really happening is that you and the elevator are falling together. Imagine the elevator is a rocket ship traveling at a great speed. You are inside, so you are traveling at the same speed. That is why you would be able to float around inside the spaceship.

You can make a model that will show why astronauts appear to float in the air.

How to Make an Astronaut That Appears to Float

Needed:

a thin wire coat hanger

a penny

Do this experiment against a playroom wall or outdoor wall.

1. Hold the hanger against the wall. Pretend the penny is an astronaut and the coat hanger is a spaceship. Put the astronaut

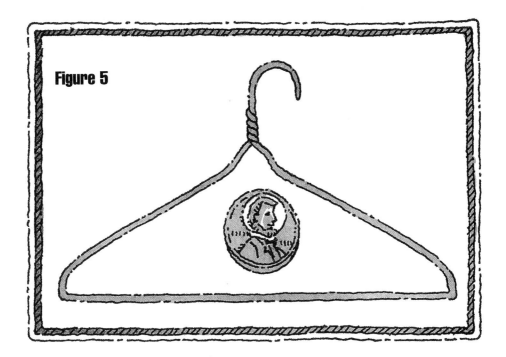

Figure 5

in the spaceship by holding the penny in the center of the hanger. The penny should not touch any part of the wire. (See Figure 5.)

2. Now release both the hanger and the penny at exactly the same time. (You may have to try several times to do this properly.) Keep your eye on the penny.

3. If you release them together, the penny will remain in the center of the coat hanger until it reaches the floor. (See Figure 6, page 20.) For those few seconds the astronaut appears to be floating in the air in the middle of the spaceship. If you had been that astronaut, you would have *felt* weightless. But actually you were being pulled by gravity all the time and were never weightless.

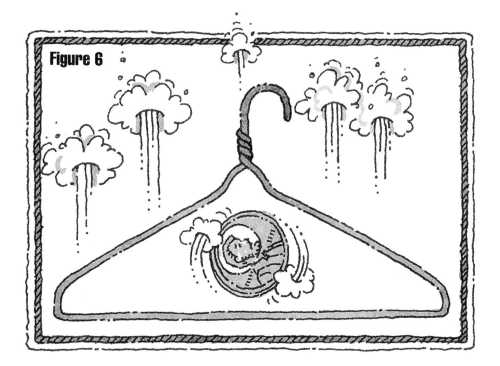

Figure 6

What Is Artificial Gravity?

But say you were an astronaut in space in a space station. You would be free of Earth's gravity. And you would be weightless. All that weightlessness might make you dizzy. That is why your space station would have **artificial gravity**. Artificial gravity is a way to keep the astronauts from feeling weightless. How does artificial gravity work? Here's an experiment to show you.

Artificial Gravity for a Penny

Needed:

the coat hanger and penny from the
previous experiment

a small piece of cardboard, about 1 inch
(2.5 centimeters) square

tape

1. Bend the hook of the hanger into a loop. (See Figure 7.)

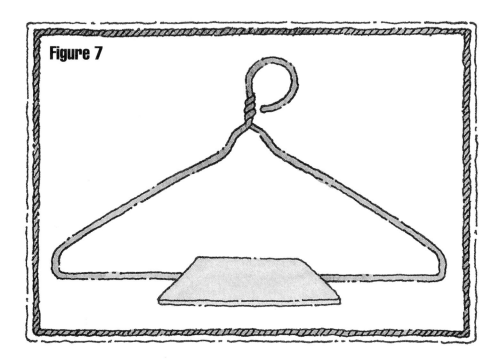

Figure 7

2. In the middle of the long bar on the bottom of the hanger tape the small piece of cardboard to make a shelf. This should be located directly below the loop.

3. Hang the loop over your forefinger and, this time, pretend the coat hanger is a space station. Set your penny astronaut in the center of the shelf. If you were to drop the hanger now, your astronaut would become weightless; but this time don't drop it. Create artificial gravity instead.

4. This will take a bit of practice, so don't give up. Start the hanger gently rocking from side to side. Then, with a quick flick, start it spinning around your finger. If you do this carefully, the penny astronaut will not fall off but will remain stuck on the shelf, even when it is upside down. (See Figure 8.)

Figure 8

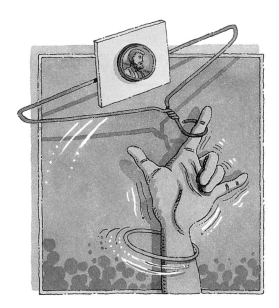

You have created artificial gravity. Let's explore how. Remember when we asked earlier in this book: Why does the moon go around Earth? We said that the moon moves in a straight line in space. And we said Earth's gravity pulls at the moon and forces it to go in a circle around the planet.

Something similar happened in this experiment. In this experiment, the penny was also moving in a straight line in space. Yet it remained on the shelf and went around your finger. Why? The hanger's spin, coupled with the shelf, did the work of Earth's gravity. Together, they held the penny in place. Together, they created artificial gravity.

Artificial gravity in a space station works the same way. The space station's spin and its walls work together to keep astronauts from being weightless.

How Do Things Fall?

We know that, because of gravity, things are always falling. But do all things fall in the same way?

Aristotle, a famous Greek philosopher who lived over 2,000 years ago, tried to answer this question. He simply said, Objects, like rocks, belong on the ground. If you lift them up and release them, they always fall back to where they belong.

And he said: Big rocks belong on the ground more than little rocks. If you drop a 10-pound (5-kilogram) rock, it will fall back to the ground ten times faster than a 1-pound (0.5-kilogram) rock.

What do you think? As far as we know, 2,000 years ago few people, including Aristotle, ever did science experiments to prove whether ideas were true. Believe it or not, nobody ever picked up two different-size rocks and dropped them to find out if the larger one fell faster—at least as far as we know.

In fact, many believe that nobody did this until nearly 2,000 years later! The Italian scientist Galileo Galilei, born in 1564, became famous by proving his ideas through experiments. He did not believe Aristotle. Galileo said: You can think of a big rock as just a lot of small rocks fastened together, and I believe that all rocks fall at the same speed.

What do you think?

Try the Experiments Aristotle Never Tried

Needed:

clay molded into three balls, all the same size

1. Hold two balls, one in each hand. Hold them side by side about even with your waist. Let them fall at exactly the same time. You will see that they fall at the same speed and strike

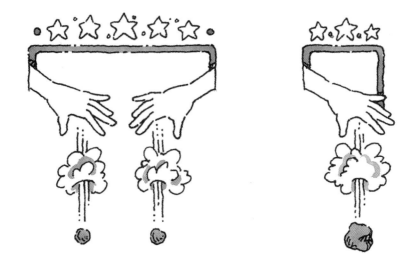

Figure 9   **Figure 10**

the ground together. (See Figure 9.) Do this several times so you know how fast they fall.

2. Squeeze the two balls together to make a single ball twice as heavy. This is what Galileo meant when he said you can think of a big rock as just a lot of little rocks joined together. Drop this larger ball and see if it seems to drop twice as fast as the small balls. (See Figure 10.) Aristotle said it should.

3. Finally, repeat step 1, but drop the big ball and the remaining small ball side by side. (See Figure 11, page 26.) If Aristotle was right, the big ball should drop twice as fast as the small

Figure 11

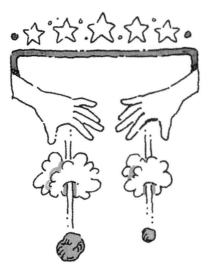

one. If Galileo was correct, they should both hit the ground at the same time.

Galileo was an experimenter. He conducted many experiments by rolling balls of different sizes and weights down ramps. (It doesn't matter whether the balls are dropped or they roll downhill. Gravity works the same.) He experimented until he was absolutely convinced he was correct. Finally, many people believe, he conducted a public demonstration to show that Aristotle was wrong and he was right. His demonstration has become famous because he did it from the Leaning Tower of Pisa in Italy. It was a perfect choice.

Because of the tower's tilt, the weights could fall to the ground without striking any part of the building. Some people, though, believe the Leaning Tower story is only a legend, and that Galileo used balls rolling down ramps to prove his theory.

So, you and Galileo proved that all objects fall at the same speed because gravity works the same way on everything, right? Well . . .

Explain This Paper Puzzler

Needed:

two sheets of paper the same size and weight

Both sheets of paper are the same size. They both weigh the same. Gravity attracts them equally. So they should both fall at exactly the same speed.

Crumple one sheet into a ball and leave the other flat. Hold one in each hand and drop them together. (See Figure 12.) What happens? The one that is crumpled will fall much faster and strike the ground long before the flat one. Why?

Before you read further, consider: Have you ever watched a leaf fall off a tree? Have you ever watched a person drop from an airplane with a parachute? They fall slowly for the

Figure 12

same reason the flat sheet of paper fell more slowly than the crumpled piece. The air slowed them down as they fell.

Although we cannot see air, it is a real substance. And, although it is not as thick as water, it acts much like water. If you had a tall glass of water and you dropped your clay ball in it, the ball would drop through the water slowly. For the ball to drop, it must push the water under it out of the way. This takes a bit of time, so a clay ball will fall more slowly in water than in air.

Likewise, air is pushed aside as objects drop through it. Because air is not as thick as water, however, it can move away faster, though it does slow down falling objects. Of course, the shape of an object determines the amount of air it has to push aside.

But this doesn't happen on the moon. There is no air on the moon. On the moon, both papers, the flat and the crumpled one, would fall at exactly the same speed. A leaf would fall just as fast as a 50-pound (23-kilogram) rock! Gravity pulls on all objects equally. It's just that on Earth the air gets in the way.

Even if you are not a parachutist, you can be thankful for the air for another reason having to do with gravity. Rain falls to the ground as gentle drops. If the air did not slow them down, falling raindrops would strike you at the speed of a bullet, and would be almost as dangerous!

Why Don't Buildings Fall Down?

If gravity pulls all objects as close to the center of the world as possible, how can we have tall buildings? Why doesn't gravity pull them down? Why doesn't gravity make us fall down?

Because we — and the buildings — are balanced. Every object has a **balancing point** in it. Scientists call this the **center of mass** or the **center of gravity**, but *balancing point* is easier for us to understand, so we will use that term as we study it. As long as an object's balancing point is as close to the ground as possible, the object is balanced, and it can't fall down any farther. Here is an easy way to find the balancing point in a ruler. The balancing point finds itself, almost like magic!

A Ruler Can Find Its Own Balancing Point

Needed:

a ruler or yardstick

1. Put your hands out in front of you with your fingers outstretched and your palms pressed against each other. Now separate your hands. Have someone set the ruler on the top of your hands so each end rests on your forefingers. Do not touch the ruler with your thumbs. (See Figure 13, page 32.)

2. Slowly move your hands toward one another. You will feel the ruler slipping, first on one hand then the other, but it

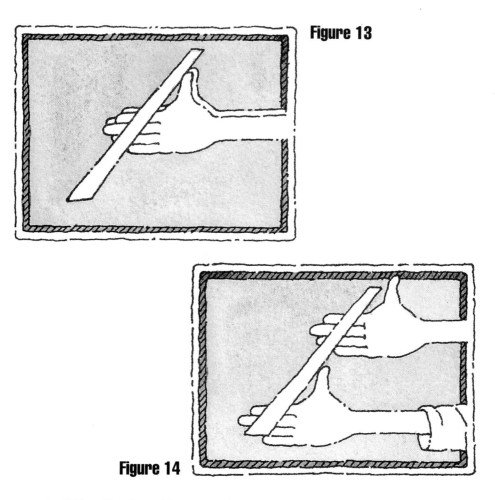

Figure 13

Figure 14

won't fall off. (See Figure 14.) Keep moving your hands together until the palms are again pressed against one another. The ruler has not fallen off, and it is balanced right in the middle. The exact center of the ruler is where its balancing point is located. (See Figure 15.) Because your hands are right

Figure 15

under the balancing point, holding up the ruler, gravity cannot make the ruler fall.

If you want to experiment further, you can change the balancing point in the ruler. Take a few coins and, using tape, attach them to one end of the ruler. Repeat the above experiment and you will find a new balancing point, closer to the coins. This is because the ruler must have equal weight on both sides of the balancing point, and the side with the coins is heavier.

You can use gravity to find the balancing point of any object. Here is an experiment that will teach you one simple way to do this.

Find the Balancing Point

Needed:

piece of cardboard about 8 inches
(20 centimeters) square

scissors

pencil

a table

Cut the cardboard into any odd shape and follow these directions to find its balancing point:

1. Set the cardboard flat on the table. Push it slowly off the tabletop until it just starts to fall. Don't let it actually fall, but when it is just about to, press your hand down on it to stop it.

2. Hold the cardboard in place. Reach under the cardboard and draw a line with your pencil along the edge of the table on the underside of the cardboard.

3. Move the cardboard back onto the table, and turn it around a little. Again push it off the edge of the table, stopping it just before it falls. Mark where the edge of the table is on its underside.

4. Do this a few more times, each time turning the cardboard a bit so the lines are in different places.

5. Turn the cardboard over and look at the lines. They all cross in one area. This is the cardboard's balancing point!

You have a balancing point. And, like the ruler, your balancing point can change. What keeps you from falling over when your balancing point changes? Your brain. It tells you—without your even being aware—how to move your body when your balancing point changes. And the message it sends you is: Keep your balancing point over your feet. As long as your balancing point remains over your feet you will not fall. But if it doesn't . . .

Figure 16

... You will fall down!

Try this experiment to see how important it is to keep your balancing point over your feet.

Needed:

a paper napkin

1. Try this: Stand with your feet together and drop the napkin on the floor in front of your toes. Now, bending your knees as little as possible, lean forward and pick up the napkin.

You probably did this easily. But, to do it, your brain had to keep your balancing point over your feet. So while your upper body tilted forward, your lower body tilted backward. This kept your hips, and your balancing point, over your feet.

2. Now try this: Stand with your back against a bare wall. Your heels should be touching the wall, too. Drop the napkin and try to pick it up, again bending your knees as little as possible. This time you can't do it without falling.

The wall prevents your lower body from moving backward, so you finally have to move your hips forward. When you do, of course, your balancing point moves forward, too, until it is no longer over your feet. That is the exact moment you start to fall. (See Figure 16.)

Because gravity is a kind of science "magic," let's finish with a balancing trick that seems to cheat gravity.

Make an "Impossible Balance" Thing

Needed:

piece of light cardboard, 3 by 5 inches
(about 8 by 13 centimeters)

scissors

two paper clips

1. Draw the shape in Figure 17 to the given dimensions on the card. Cut the shape out of the card. Try to balance the point on the tip of your finger. It will fall off.

2. Next attach one clip to each "wing" as shown in Figure 18 and try to balance the card again. This time it balances, even though it looks as though it should fall off. (See Figure 19, page 40.) If you try carefully, you can even balance it on a sharp pencil eraser—which really looks impossible!

Of course you now know the secret. Your finger, or the pencil point, is right under the balancing point. Even though the

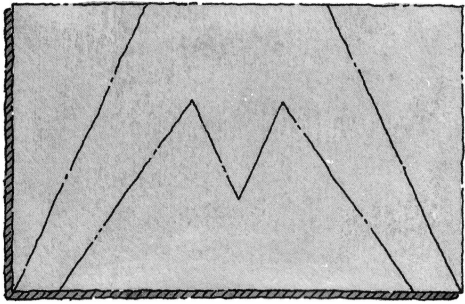

Figure 17

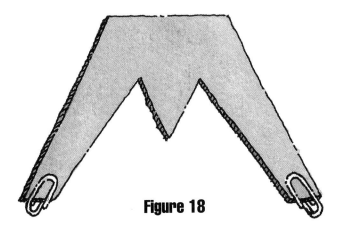

Figure 18

Figure 19

heavy paper clips look like they should make the thing fall down, they can't. In fact, although it looks very mysterious, the thing is held in place by gravity, not magic!

Speaking of magic, have you ever watched a magician float someone in the air? If you watched in amazement it means that you already know a lot about gravity. You know that gravity is everywhere and, unless something is holding an object up, the object falls down. The magician's floating-person trick puzzles everyone because we learn about gravity from the moment we are born. Even little children know they fall down and never fall "up," and know they cannot float in the air. The magician seems to defy gravity, and that is impossible. But gravity, as we've seen, is a kind of "magic" too.

Glossary

artificial gravity   gravity created by spinning a falling object.

balancing point (also known as the **center of mass** or the **center of gravity**)   the point of an object that is closest to the ground, where the object's weight is equal on all sides.

force   a push or pull on an object.

gravity   a force that pulls things downward.

universal law of gravity   an idea proposed by Sir Isaac Newton that states that every body, no matter how large or small, possesses gravity.

Further Reading

Branley, Franklyn M. *Gravity Is a Mystery.* New York: Harper-Collins, 1986.

Nardo, Don. *Gravity: The Universal Force.* San Diego: Lucent, 1990.

Taylor, Barbara. *Weight and Balance.* New York: Franklin Watts, 1990.

Index

About the Author

In first grade Larry White became fascinated with magic, and in high school he became fascinated with science.

Today, Larry is director of the Needham Elementary Science Center in Massachusetts, where he has taught young children for the last twenty-nine years. Before that, he was employed by the Education Department of Boston's Museum of Science. Larry has written a dozen books for curious young scientists.

Larry is also the magic editor of the magazine of the Society of American Magicians. He creates and describes magic tricks for professional magicians. He has also written over a dozen books for curious young magicians.

Larry believes that his interests in magic and science go together because things that appear magical can often be explained scientifically, if people are curious and willing to experiment and investigate.